D0783745

This edition published 2005 by
Mercury Books
20 Bloomsbury Street
London WC1B 3JH
ISBN 1-904668-77-1
Copyright © 2003 Allegra Publishing Ltd

Publisher: Felicia Law
Design director: Tracy Carrington
Project manager: Karen Foster
Author: Gerry Bailey
Editor: Rosalind Beckman
Designed by: Jacqueline Palmer
assisted by Simon Brewster, Will Webster
Cartoon illustrations: Steve Boulter (Advocate)
Make-and-do: Jan Smith
Model-maker: Tim Draper
Photo studio: Steve Lumb
Photo research: Diana Morris
Scanning: Imagewrite
Digital workflow: Edward MacDermott

Printed by D 2 Print Singapore

BROMLEY PUBLIC LIBRARIES	
02654888	
PET	24-Oct-05
608	£7.99
BHIJUN	

Photo Credits
H. & J. Blackwell/Trip: 17t. Steve Brock/Eye Ubiquitous: 30b.
James Davis Travel Photography: 29t. J. Ellard/Trip: 38b.
P. M. Field/Eye Ubiquitous: 9t. W. Jacobs/Trip: 26b.
Darren Maybury/Eye Ubiquitous: 33t. John Miles/Eye Ubiquitous: 37t.
Brian Mitchell/Photofusion: 14t. Gianni Dagli Orti/Corbis: 42b.
Chris Parker/Hutchison Picture Library: 21t. Topham Picturepoint: 22b.
Picturesque/Trip: 10b. Roger Ressmeyer/Corbis: 13t.
H. Rogers/Trip: 5t. Paul Seheult/Eye Ubiquitous: 34b.
Dr Nigel Smith/Hutchison: 25t. G Stokoe/Trip: 18b.
Trip: 41t. Graham Wheatley/Eye Ubiquitous: 6b.

Crafty Inventions

GREAT INVENTORS

Contents

Mercury Junior

20 Bloomsbury Street
London WC1B 3JH

Why is Archimedes so famous?

A Greek mathematician and inventor who lived between 287 and 212 BC, Archimedes became the greatest scientist in the ancient world. He also studied geometry and physics, and made important discoveries in each. His weapons of war were used to defend Syracuse against the Romans.

Archimedes was born in Syracuse, a city ruled by Greece, in Sicily. He grew up with a keen interest in mathematics and the world around him.

But the best place to study Greek culture was not in Greece, but in Egypt. So Archimedes moved to Alexandria, a great centre of learning.

Just watch! I'm going to show you how easy it is to lift things that are incredibly heavy.

He was inspired by another Greek mathematician called Euclid. At the end of his studies, Archimedes returned to Syracuse where he did much of his work for King Hiero II.

WHAT DID HE DO?

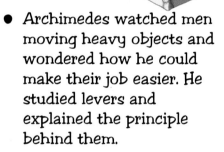

● Archimedes watched men moving heavy objects and wondered how he could make their job easier. He studied levers and explained the principle behind them.

● Then he boasted to King Hiero that he could move the Earth. In other words, that people could move objects many times heavier than themselves if they used a lever or a pulley.

● So King Hiero challenged Archimedes to prove his claim. Archimedes set up a system of pulleys, which he attached to a ship. The ship was loaded with passengers and freight. To the king's astonishment, Archimedes moved the ship all by himself!

Eureka! I've discovered the principle of buoyancy. An object floating in a liquid seems to lose an amount of weight equal to the weight of the fluid it displaces. So a ship displaces an amount of water equal to its own weight, which is why it floats.

Archimedes made his famous discovery of the principles of displacement while he was taking a bath.

Cheating the king

King Hiero once suspected that a goldsmith had cheated him by adding silver to a crown that should have been made of pure gold. He asked Archimedes to find out whether the goldsmith was a fraud. Archimedes thought about the problem, but he only solved it when he got into a bath that had been filled up to the brim. He noticed that water spilled out of the bath when he placed his body into it.

He measured the amount of water and found that its volume weighed the same as his body. Archimedes then measured the amount of water displaced, or spilled, by the crown when he dropped it into the bath, and the amount displaced by an equal weight of pure gold. The crown displaced more water as the added silver had made it heavier. The goldsmith had indeed swindled the king and was beheaded for his crime!

Useful devices

Archimedes is considered to be one of the best mathematicians of all time. In geometry, he worked on calculating the area of objects with curved lines or surfaces. This is called exhaustion and is much like calculus, a method used in mathematics today.

His studies formed the basis for the science called hydrostatics, or the study of liquids at rest. His discovery that submerged objects displace a volume of liquid equal to their weight and become lighter by exactly the weight they displace is called the Archimedes principle. He invented many useful devices based on his discoveries. His Archimedes screw was a type of pump used for irrigation, and it is still used in some parts of the world today. He invented levers and pulleys that could lift great weights, and built cranes and other devices to defend Syracuse against the Roman army.

FALL OF SYRACUSE

Syracuse and Rome were at war because Rome wanted the city to become part of her empire. When it was finally captured, the Roman general, Marcellus, ordered that its citizens should not be harmed. But one soldier did not obey. He killed Archimedes while the inventor worked on a geometry problem.

Archimedes used a compass and other geometry instruments when planning the defenses of Syracuse.

Inventor's words

calculus
exhaustion
hydrostatics
volume

Make a diving duo

You will need

- clay • blunt knife for modelling clay
- acrylic paints and brush
- clear acetate • scissors
- permanent marker pen
- polyboard or stiff card
- coloured drawing pin
- food wrap
- PVA glue

1 Model a bathtub from clay and attach 2 pairs of clay legs. Leave to dry, then paint.

2 Cut out a large circle of acetate and make a hole in the centre. Draw 2 divers on the back of the disc with your marker pen and paint them.

3 Decorate a piece of scored polyboard to look like the inside of a bathroom, with splashes of water.

4 Attach the acetate disc to the backboard with a drawing pin. You should be able to spin the disc with your finger.

5 Position your bathtub so that it almost touches the backboard. Stick a piece of acetate over the top of the bath so it looks full of water and add food wrap for splashes.

Artist, scientist – and inventor, too?

Leonardo da Vinci was a man of many talents. Considered one of the greatest inventors of all time, he was also a brilliant artist and sculptor who studied anatomy, architecture, engineering and other sciences. Born in 1452 at Vinci, in Italy, from where he took his name, Leonardo died in France in 1519.

In 1482, Leonardo moved from Vinci to Milan, where he became state engineer. His town planning may have helped halt the spread of the plague two years later.

When a French army invaded Milan, he he moved to Florence where he became architect and engineer to Cesare Borgia, the son of the Pope.

In 1516, he left Italy and settled in France, where he lived as the guest of the French King, He filled over 40 notebooks with ideas and sketches. After his death, some were lost and lay undiscovered for 400 years.

I just can't make up my mind! Shall I be a painter, inventor, doctor, mathematician, architect. . .?

WHAT DID HE DECIDE?

- Well, he became all of them! Many of Leonardo's ideas were written down in notebooks. Over 4000 pages have survived.

- Leonardo spent so much time perfecting his work, that some pieces were left unfinished. His *Mona Lisa* took four years to paint.

- Fascinated by human anatomy, he dissected more than 30 corpses, and made many drawings of his observations..

- His designs for the helicopter, plane and submarine were hundreds of years ahead of their time, although not all of them would have worked.

I'm bursting with ideas! We must protect our cities with better weapons. So I have designed an armoured vehicle that moves on wheels, and a mortar gun that can fire large objects. My guns will have rifled barrels so the bullets will fly straight.

Leonardo spent a lot of time designing war machines because the city states of Italy often fought against each other.

'Modern' ideas

Leonardo invented so many things, that no single one stands out. He was interested in flight and birds, so he designed a flying machine and a **parachute**. The parachute would have worked, while the flying machine showed that he knew the basic principles of **aerodynamics**, or streamlining, and **lift**. He was also interested in underwater exploration.

He drew a diving suit with a special helmet for breathing, and left notes and sketches for a series of tools and devices. These used the elements of simple machines, including screws, pulleys, gears, levers and **ratchets**, a toothed device that allows one-way movement only. Before he died, Leonardo apologised to 'God and Man for leaving so much undone'!

Renaissance

When Leonardo was born, a brilliant new movement was taking place in Europe, called the Renaissance, which means rebirth. People were bursting with new ideas and re-learning old, forgotten ones. The arts were flourishing, and there were enormous advances in science, engineering and medicine. Leonardo became a symbol of the Renaissance.

The Renaissance was helped by the fall of the Byzantine city of Constantinople to the Ottoman Turks. Constantinople was a city of learning and after it fell, many classical books were transported to Italy. In Germany, the printing press had been invented, allowing these books to be printed and distributed amongst many more ordinary people. In the meantime, a new class of merchants and bankers were making their fortunes. This was important for artists and scientists such as Leonardo, who relied on their sponsorship.

Leonardo's portrait, the Mona Lisa, became famous because of her mysterious smile and her calm and graceful appearance.

BACK TO FRONT

Leonardo planned to write books on the subjects he'd studied. But he only got as far as writing notes in his notebooks. However, to make sure no one copied his ideas, he wrote in code with his left hand. He used a kind of reversed writing, or mirror writing. This was even used to write his instructions for a stink bomb - one of Leonardo's practical jokes.

Inventor's words

aerodynamics
lift
parachute
ratchet
Renaissance

Make a corkscrew helicopter

You will need

- PVA glue • plastic bowl
- large plastic lid
- plastic bottle • scissors
- bendable wire
- cardboard tube
- 3 polystyrene cups
- coloured card and paper
- double-sided tape
- kebab stick • metallic card
- paints and brush
- sticker stars

1 Glue the lid to the bowl. Now cut the top off a plastic bottle and glue that to the lid.

2 Wrap 3 pieces of wire around a tube, to make springs. Cut off the bottoms of 3 cups and tape each spring to a cup, then attach the springs to the base of the lid, as shown. Make a hole in the bottle lid and slide in a kebab stick.

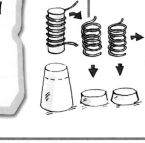

3 Cut out a small, medium and large circle from coloured card. Make a hole in the middle of each. Cut from the rim to the centre of each disc. Now glue one end of the small disc to one end of the medium disc, then one end of the medium disc to one end of the large disc.

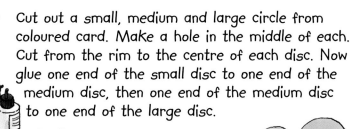

4 Slide the 3-disc screw on to a tube of paper that fits neatly into the central hole. Trim the screw edges for an even shape and glue to fix.

5 Wedge pieces of polystyrene into the paper tube and push down over the kebab stick so the screw is fixed to the main body. Stick on little chairs made from folded card. Paint and decorate.

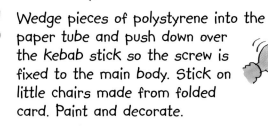

11

Who invented the printing press?

Although he was trained as a goldsmith, Johannes Gutenberg was also a printer, who invented a new type of press in 1430. His machine changed the world of learning because books were easily copied and so had a wider readership. He was born in Mainz, Germany, in 1400, and died there in 1468.

Ever since the invention of writing, copying scrolls or books had been a pain-staking business. Often it was done by teams of scribes in monasteries.

They spent a long time illuminating, or decorating, the books. Although beautiful, these books took for ever to make. There had to be a quicker way.

Copying books by hand is slow and boring. I need a machine that will print many copies at the same time.

The Chinese and Koreans had developed a system of printing with wood – and even ceramic – blocks. But their languages were complex and required too many characters. The system was just too difficult to use.

WHAT DID HE DO?

- The Chinese had invented moveable type. The letters were cut out individually and moved around to make words.

- But this took up a lot of time. Surely there was a way of speeding up the process. Wasn't there?

- Johannes wanted to fix all the letters of a complete page in one place, ink them and press them - all at the same time.

- So he devised metal type that was fixed into wooden blocks. The blocks could be fitted into a plate, or bed. So far, so good. But what about the pressing?

I know! I'll use the same system as a wine press. I'll put a flat piece of wood at the end of the screw bit. Then I'll spread ink on the type and place paper on top. When the press is screwed down, it will print a whole page.

Gutenberg's printing press increased the number of books available to ordinary people.

Fast printing

Johannes Gutenberg's **printing press** can truly be called a world-changing invention. Using his press, Gutenberg could print more material in a day than a **scribe** could copy in a year. Hundreds more books could be produced, and in large quantities. This lowered the price of printed matter, which then became readily available to ordinary people.

Gutenberg's genius was fixing pieces of type on to wooden **blocks**, which were fitted into a **bed**. Then, using the wine press idea, he added a moveable piece of wood called a **platen** to the end of the screw. The platen pressed the paper on to the inked type. This meant a whole page could be printed at once, instead of pressing one letter at a time.

Letter-setter

Johannes Gutenberg came from an aristocratic family named Gensfleisch. But we know him by his mother's name, which he always used.

As an aristocrat, Johannes did not have to serve an apprenticeship and may have learned metalwork from his uncle who was master of the mint at Mainz. His skills allowed him to experiment with a new kind of instrument called a **type mould**. The type mould produced types that could be **ranged**, or laid, in even lines. They were then locked together by wedges called **quoins**, to make up a unit known as a **forme**. Formes with hundreds of letters could easily be put on to, and removed from, the press. Ink for the press was made from materials similar to those used by early Dutch painters.

FASTER AND FASTER

Since the first printing presses, printing has become incredibly fast. Newspapers, which have to be printed very quickly, are reeled off at 30,000 copies every hour. But the most rapid presses can print the entire Bible, which contains nearly 800,000 words, in just over a minute!

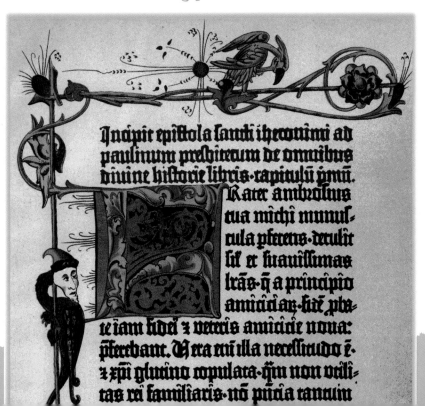

A decorative page from the Gutenberg Bible, printed in Latin in 1457. The type is upright, each letter having pointed feet and few curves.

Inventor's words

bed • block
forme • platen
printing press
quoin
range • scribe
type mould

Make your own prints

You will need

- pencil
- thick card or foamboard (A3-size)
- thin string • scissors
- paints and brush
- strong glue
- sheets of cartridge paper (A3-size) • rolling pin

1 Draw a simple outline of a picture on the card or foamboard.

2 Using your outline as a guide, build up the picture by gluing on pieces of string. Pattern each part of your picture differently for a varied textural effect.

3 Quickly paint over your string picture – the paint has to be wet in order to print.

4 Place a piece of cartridge paper on top of the wet string and press down on it with a rolling pin several times to transfer the paint evenly on to the paper.

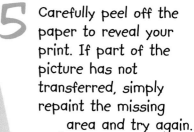

5 Carefully peel off the paper to reveal your print. If part of the picture has not transferred, simply repaint the missing area and try again.

Who invented the wireless?

Born in Bologna, Italy, in 1874, Guglielmo Marconi studied physics and went on to develop wireless telegraphy, or radio, communications. He discovered that radio waves could be transmitted and received over long distances. He died in Rome in 1937.

After schooling in Bologna and Florence, Guglielmo attended the technical school in Leghorn where he became fascinated by electromagnetic waves.

He was especially interested in radio waves, as scientist Heinrich Herz had found out how to transmit and receive them. over very short distances.

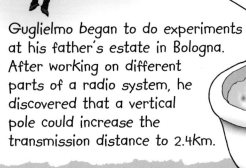

Make fun of me if you like, but I will prove that radio waves can be transmitted over huge distances!

Guglielmo began to do experiments at his father's estate in Bologna. After working on different parts of a radio system, he discovered that a vertical pole could increase the transmission distance to 2.4km.

WHAT HAPPENED NEXT?

- Some scientists laughed at the idea that radio waves could be transmitted over long distances. Frustrated, Guglielmo moved to England.

- There he demonstrated his radio transmissions successfully . He even tied aerials to balloons and kites to make his radio signals travel further.

- He was able to transmit signals up to 14.5km. Eventually, he showed that radio signals could be sent from land to ships at sea.

- But he was snubbed by scientists who said that the curvature of the Earth would always limit the transmission of radio waves to 322km.

Well, I was right and you were wrong! I set up a receiving station in Canada and transmitted from England. The signals were received on the other side of the Atlantic, which proves that the Earth's curve doesn't limit distance.

Marconi transmitting wireless waves across the Atlantic, from Cornwall to Newfoundland.

Across the Atlantic

When Guglielmo Marconi proved that radio waves could be transmitted across the Atlantic Ocean in 1901, his discovery caused a huge sensation all over the world. His inventions allowed electromagnetic, or radio, waves to be sent over long distances without using wires. This is why the system was originally called wireless telegraphy.

Marconi's receiver was first called a wireless, then a radio. He found that radio waves could be sent much further if they were concentrated in a beam by reflectors and an aerial. His work on aerials showed that radio communications could be worldwide. He received many prizes for his work, including the Nobel Prize for physics in 1909.

Aerial power

A radio transmitter sends out radio waves at a certain fixed frequency. Frequency is the number of waves per second. These waves are called carrier waves and are picked up by a receiver some distance away. The sound to be sent, such as a voice or music, is changed into electrical signals by the transmitter and combined with the carrier wave. When the carrier wave is picked up by the receiver, the electrical signals are decoded into sound again.

Guglielmo Marconi found that the strength of the signal being sent could be increased if the carrier wave was passed to an aerial and beamed through the atmosphere towards a receiver. Radio waves were first sent as short wave, long wave and medium wave signals. But today, most people receive VHF and UHF, which stand for Very High Frequency and Ultra High Frequency. These waves can be sent via a satellite.

STAY TUNED!

Take a look at a radio and you will see many numbers on the display panel at the front. These numbers stand for a particular frequency. Each radio station uses its own frequency to transmit its sounds. So when you tune into the frequency number, you always get the same station.

A DJ transmits his music through a certain frequency. Most radiostations are known by their frequency number.

Inventor's words

aerial
carrier wave
electromagnetic wave
frequency
wireless
telegraphy

Make a radar helmet

You will need

- balloon • newspaper strips • PVA glue
- thin wire, kebab sticks, foil cake tins, bottle tops
- plastic margarine tub lid
- scissors • foil
- elastic band or card strap
- metallic paint and brush
- metallic card, sticker stars, sequins

1 Cover the top half of the balloon with layers of newspaper strips soaked in PVA glue.

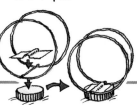

2 Make aerials and mini satellite dishes from wire, kebab sticks, cake tins and bottle tops.

3 Make a large dish for the front of the helmet from a tub lid, bottle top, kebab stick and wire, as shown.

4 Pop the balloon and trim the edges of the paper hat. Cover the hat in foil and glue on the aerials and dishes.

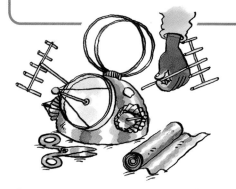

5 Attach an elastic band or card strap to the hat. Paint and decorate the hat with metallic card, stickers and sequins.

Who improved the steam engine?

Richard Trevithick was born in 1771. He was a British engineer whose work in the tin mines of Cornwall fuelled his interest in steam engines. These were used to pump water from the mines. Trevithick built the first steam-powered road vehicle and then, in 1804, the first steam-powered railway locomotive.

Richard went to school in a small village where his teacher described him as 'disobedient, slow and obstinate'. But the boy had a special talent - an aptitude for engineering. He could solve problems that defeated even well-educated engineers.

WHAT DID HE DO?

- James Watt had designed the steam engines the miners used. He thought an engine powered by 'strong' steam would be too dangerous.

- But Trevithick was obstinate and refused to change his mind.

- He believed that by using high-pressure steam and allowing it to expand, or get bigger, in the cylinder, he could create a much smaller and lighter engine with just as much power.

- Mr. Watt disapproved of Trevithick's plans. In fact, he said that Trevithick deserved hanging for bringing such an engine into use. Who was right?

I'm going to make a lightweight engine that uses high-pressure steam without bursting the boiler!

By the age of 19, he was engineer to several mining firms. At that time, miners worked huge steam engines that used steam at low pressure. But they weren't efficient. The miners needed something better...

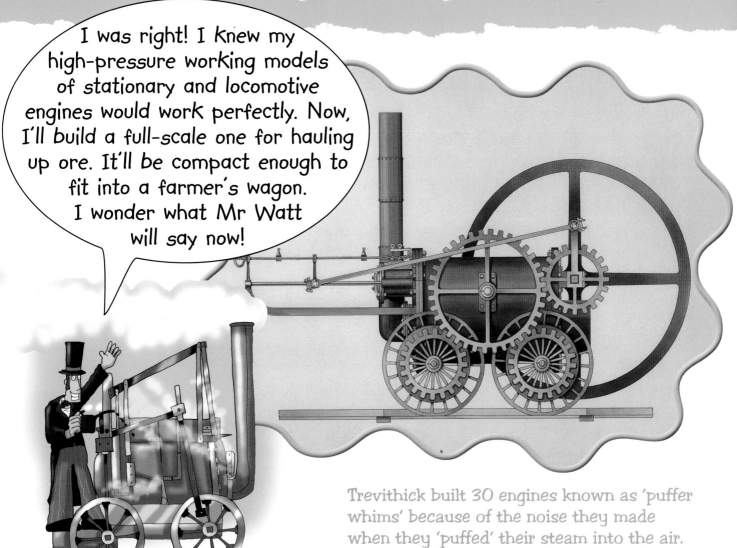

I was right! I knew my high-pressure working models of stationary and locomotive engines would work perfectly. Now, I'll build a full-scale one for hauling up ore. It'll be compact enough to fit into a farmer's wagon. I wonder what Mr Watt will say now!

Trevithick built 30 engines known as 'puffer whims' because of the noise they made when they 'puffed' their steam into the air.

Under pressure

Trevithick's **high-pressure steam engine** was his greatest invention. It led to the development of the steam **locomotive** – and the railway system. The steam engine had been developed by James Watt. But it was huge and heavy. What's more, it wasn't that efficient, which was a problem for the Cornish tin miners. Since there were no coal mines in Cornwall, coal had to be imported, so using a steam engine was costly.

Something had to be done, and Trevithick had the answer. He didn't believe **high-pressure** steam would be dangerous, as others at the time believed. Eventually, his stubborn personality proved them all wrong. Trevithick's steam engine was smaller, more efficient and cost the miners much less to operate. It was soon in great demand for lifting men, ore and refuse up mine shafts right across the country.

Steam machines

Richard Trevithick's high-pressure steam engines resulted in an expansion of steam power that would not have been possible with Watt's original engine. Richard wanted to use the engine not just for stationary power but as a power plant, or motor, for moving things, such as carts and carriages.

Trevithick's first steam vehicle was a carriage. On Christmas Eve, 1801, he successfully drove the carriage up a hill near his home. Two years later, he built a second one, which he drove through the streets of London. The following year he built a steam railway locomotive at an ironworks belonging to Samuel Pomfrey. Pomfrey won a bet when the locomotive hauled 10 tons of iron and 70 men along 16km of the normally horse-drawn tramway – proper railway lines had yet to be built.

UNLUCKY GENIUS

Trevithick might have been a brilliant engineer, but he was hopeless with money. While he was building engines for copper and silver mines in Peru, he got caught up in wars there and lost a fortune. By the time he returned home, the Stephensons had become famous for building locomotives and had profited from his genius. He died in poverty in 1833 and was buried in an unmarked grave.

Trevithick's steam carriage was a monster in its day.

Inventor's words

high pressure
steam engine
locomotive
power plant

Make your own locomotive

You will need

- thick cardboard
- scissors, craft knife
- cardboard tube
- PVA glue • box lids
- coloured card
- paint and brush
- bottle top • cane
- washing-up liquid bottle lid
- small box
- wire • cotton wool

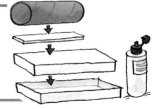

1 Glue a strip of thick card to the bottom of the tube and stick this on to 2 box lids stuck together.

2 Make a train cabin from coloured card, as shown. Stick on a cardboard roof.

3 Decorate your engine. Make a funnel by sticking a bottle top on to a roll of card, then stick a card disc over the train's boiler unit.

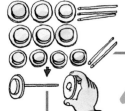

4 Cut out 6 circles of thick card and glue them to slightly larger circles of thin card. Make 2 pairs of smaller wheels in the same way.

5 Glue a small box to the front of the underside of the engine and fix all the sets of wheels. Attach a bent piece of wire and cotton wool to the funnel for smoke.

What led to the electric motor?

Although he had little formal education, Michael Faraday became a respected scientist. He studied both chemistry and physics, and discovered the principle of electromagnetic induction. This eventually led to the invention of the electric motor. He was born in 1791 and died in 1867.

Michael was brought up in a village near London. His father was a poor blacksmith, and often he and his brothers had very little to eat.

Although he didn't go to school, he learned to read and write. At 14, he was apprenticed to a bookbinder. The books inspired a lively interest in science.

WHAT DID HE DO?

- At the Royal Institution, he worked with the most important scientists of the day. He also became a master of laboratory techniques.

- He was so impressive that he was often paid to be a witness at legal trials where he would analyse evidence.

- His discoveries led him to believe that he could make a current in a wire using a magnet, because they both involved forces.

- In time, he produced a continuous current by spinning a wired-up copper disc between the poles of a magnet. Michael had made the first dynamo.

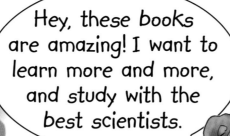

Hey, these books are amazing! I want to learn more and more, and study with the best scientists.

He began experimenting with electricity and made a simple battery. His enthusiasm led to a job with Sir Humphrey Davy, a famous chemist at the Royal Institution in London. He stayed there for 54 years.

If I reverse the process of the dynamo, I can get the copper disc to spin. The spinning disc, or a rod, can be attached to a machine to work it. It'll be the first electric motor!

A dynamo, or generator, used in a car. As long as the car is moving, the generator will produce electricity.

Creating a current

A **generator**, or **dynamo**, is an electricity-making machine. It uses magnetism to generate, or create, an electric current. Michael Faraday discovered that when a wire moves inside inside a **magnetic field**, or the lines of magnetism that stretch between its north and south poles, an electric current flows inside the wire.

His simple discovery changed the way people looked at electricity and how it could be created. Faraday used his discovery to make a generator. This kind of mechanical engine makes a coil of wire rotate in the magnetic field created by a specially-shaped magnet. As the coil turns, an electric current flows in the wire.

Hydroelectrics

Hydroelectricity is electricity that is generated from water. It might come from a dam, a waterfall or even the tide. The force from the flow of water is used to power a generator.

The energy from the water comes from movement and is known as kinetic energy. As the water flows, it turns a turbine, which is like a huge propeller. But instead of the propeller pushing an object forward, the force of water against it makes it turn. Connected to the propeller is a shaft that drives a big generator. The generator works in the same way as a small one does in a car, except it can create a lot more electricity. Hydroelectric stations can make enough electric energy to supply whole cities. The plant at Niagara in Canada supplies most of the electricity for the province of Ontario, serving millions of people.

The Hydroelectric plant at Niagara.

CHRISTMAS LECTURE

Michael Faraday believed that teaching young people about science was very important. He was a superb lecturer, and every Christmas between 1826 and 1861, he gave lectures for children at the Royal Institution. His most famous lecture was called 'The Chemical History of a Candle'. The Christmas Lectures still take place today.

Inventor's words

dynamo
generator
hydroelectricity
kinetic energy
magnetic field

Make your own motor

You will need

- copper wire
- hammer and nails
- rectangular piece of board
- 2 C-batteries
- polystyrene cup
- empty toilet roll
- strong glue
- circular magnets
- sticky tape

1 Coil a long strip of wire around itself 5 times and leave the ends sticking out, as shown.

2 Ask a grown-up to help you knock nails into a board around 2 batteries. The batteries must be tightly connected.

3 Glue a cup to the top of a toilet roll, as shown. Put 2 magnets on top of the cup and 3 inside it – magnetism will hold them in place. Glue the toilet roll to the board.

4 Force a piece of wire between a nail and the battery contact. Trail it along the board and up the cup tower, taping it to the side. Then trail the wire above the cup and make a small loop. Repeat this process from the other nail, as shown.

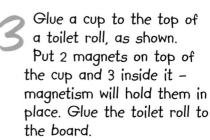

5 Thread the ends of the copper coil into the loop above the cup tower, making sure the bottom of the coil is only just above the magnets by 1–2mm.

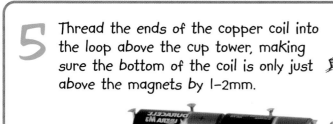

Who invented the telephone?

Like his father, Alexander Bell was an expert in elocution and speech correction. But he is best known for his work with the deaf and the invention of the telephone. Born in Edinburgh, Scotland, in 1847, he and his family later moved to Canada. He died in Nova Scotia in 1922.

Alexander was trained from a young age to follow in his father's footsteps. He spent some time at school but was mostly educated at home.

He became a teacher at Weston House Academy where he first became interested in sound. He taught music and elocution.

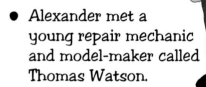

WHAT DID HE DO NEXT?

- Alexander met a young repair mechanic and model-maker called Thomas Watson.

- Together, they worked on new ideas about sound and electricity. Alexander was sure sound could be transmitted using electricity. But how?

- The two men spent long nights on their experiments and devices. Slowly but surely, their work began to pay off.

- They used sound to make a soft iron diaphragm vibrate. The vibrations caused a disturbance in the magnetic field of a bar magnet. Could they make the same happen in a copper wire?

Help! I'm not short of ideas, but I do need someone who's mechanically-minded to build my machines.

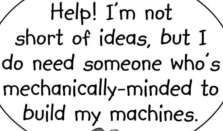

After moving to Canada, Alexander then settled in Boston, USA, where he taught deaf children to speak. He continued his experiments with sound, and was particularly fascinated by how sound could be transmitted mechanically.

Well. the vibration DID make a disturbance in copper wire, so we set up a transmitter and receiver in different rooms. Then I spilled acid from a battery on my clothes. 'Mr. Watson, come here. I want you!' I said. And Watson heard every word!

Alexander Bell with his telephone in 1876. He was inspired in his work by his wife and mother, who were both deaf.

Vibrations

Alexander Graham Bell's most famous invention was the **telephone**. He didn't think of it as a telephone at first, but rather a kind of super **telegraph**. In fact, the patent for the machine called it 'one that transmitted vocal or other sounds telegraphically'. Bell's main aim in inventing the device was to make communicating over distances easier.

He used his knowledge of how sound travelled in waves, and how these waves could make things **vibrate**. His problem was making the vibrations work with electricity, so he observed how **magnetic fields** affected electric currents. What he learned made it possible for him to invent the telephone – changing the way people communicate for ever.

Sound devices

When Alexander Graham Bell invented the telephone, it was really just a beginning. He came up with many more ideas, including the graphophone.

In 1880, with money he had been given for winning the French Volta Prize, he built the Volta Laboratory in Washington. Here, with the help of Charles Tainter and Chichester Bell, he invented the graphophone. This used a wax cylinder and discs with an engraver's stylus, and was an early kind of recording machine, similar to a record player. Alexander continued to experiment with the transmission of sound and invented another device called a photophone, which transmitted sound on a beam of light. Much of Alexander's work was ahead of its time. A century later, the principles behind his photophone led to fibre optics technology, which sends huge amounts of information around the world today.

EXPANDING NETWORK

The first telephone exchange opened in New Haven in America in 1878. There were just 21 lines and each one had to be linked by hand. The first long-distance line ran between Boston and New York. By 1887, there were more than 100,000 telephone owners. Today, there are over 600 million worldwide.

Early Bell Telephone switchboard operators.

Inventor's words

graphophone
magnetic field
photophone
telegraph
telephone
vibrate

Make your own megaphone

You will need

- thin coloured and white card
- thick card
- double-sided tape
- coloured paper
- pencil • scissors
- PVA glue

1 Roll a piece of red card into a cone shape and fix with double-sided tape. Trim the large end so it is straight all the way round.

2 Put the open end of the cone over a piece of pink paper and draw around it. Now draw a large pair of lips around the circle. Make sure you cut some tabs on the inside of the circle so you can stick it to the end of the cone.

3 Cut out a set of toothy pieces, with tabs, from white card.

4 Cut a tongue from red card and fix it into the mouth at the front and back so that it stands up slightly in the middle. Make some tonsils and tape them to the back of the cone.

5 Use thick card to make a handle for your megaphone and tape to fix.

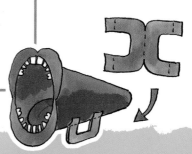

31

Who switched on the light?

One of the most productive inventors of his time, Thomas Alva Edison, was born in 1847 in the USA. He worked on projects ranging from telegraphy to antisubmarine weapons, and took out over 1000 patents in his lifetime. But Edison is best known for inventing the lightbulb. He died in 1931.

Thomas had only three months of schooling. He was educated by his mother, who encouraged his love of learning. Thomas began to read as much as he could.

When he was 15, a railroad accident left him partially deaf. So he learned how to use a telegraph and soon became a full-time telegraph operator.

WHAT DID HE DO?

- Thomas moved to New York where he worked in partnership with several people. He concentrated on the telegraph business as companies fought to find better and better equipment.

- As an independent inventor, Thomas worked for whoever paid him the most money. At Western Union he invented the quadruplex, a telegraph system that could send four messages over one wire.

- But in 1874, a bitter rival of the company offered Thomas $100,000 for the invention and snatched it from under Western Union's nose. Even with the money, Thomas had financial problems. So he decided to have a word with his father.

I want to invent something really special – something that'll light up people's lives!

During this time he used much of his energy to improve equipment and invent devices to compensate for his deafness. He became so successful that he gave up his job and became a full-time inventor.

I know, I'll bring my father to Menlo Park in New Jersey. He can help *build* a laboratory and machine shop there, where I can work with my assistants. That'll mean I can concentrate on inventing, and not worry about money!

Thomas Edison showing the world his newfangled phonograph machine, invented in 1878.

Light bulb

While Thomas worked on inventions for transmitting sound, great steps were being taken in the development of electric **arc lights**. This light came from an electric spark in the form of an arc that crossed between two conductors. Arc lights were fine for street lamps, but they were too powerful for the home. Thomas thought that it might be possible to reduce the intense light

made by the arc light inside a burner, or bulb. The problem was to prevent the bulb melting with the heat. After many experiments, a glass **vacuum bulb**, or one with the air taken out, worked. When a current was passed through a tiny string of carbon inside the bulb, it glowed. Thomas had invented the **electric light bulb**.

Movies

Although Thomas Edison is known for many inventions, he was also one of the fathers of the motion picture industry. After developing the phonograph, Thomas wanted to investigate whether he could link it to pictures that appeared to move. It seemed a great idea.

With the help of William K. L. Dickson, Thomas built a camera and a viewing device. He called them the kinetograph and kinetoscope. Unfortunately, Thomas couldn't find a way to link sound with motion, or movement, so the brilliant idea had to wait. Still, he constructed the first motion picture stage in his laboratory and made moving pictures, which marked the beginning of the silent film age. His kinetoscopes, which had peepholes where one person at a time could view the moving picture, became very popular.

Kinetoscopes were popular until rival inventors produced screen-projection systems.

A $30,000 BOAST

How to make an electric light had perplexed inventors for years. But Thomas Edison was so sure of himself, he boasted that he would invent 'a safe, mild and inexpensive light to replace the gas light'.

His past work was so highly regarded, that several financiers together advanced him $30,000 to make good his boast. And he did just that!

Inventor's words

arc light
electric light bulb
kinetograph
kinetoscope
phonograph
vacuum bulb

Mega bulb lampshade

You will need

- thick and thin bendable wire
- thin card
- scissors
- elastic band
- crêpe paper
- PVA glue

1 Shape the outline of a huge light *bulb* with thick, bendable wire. Make 3 more, copying the shape of the first. Make inward-facing hooks at both ends of each *bulb* shape.

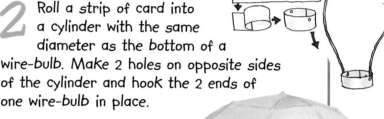

2 Roll a strip of card into a cylinder with the same diameter as the bottom of a wire-bulb. Make 2 holes on opposite sides of the cylinder and hook the 2 ends of one wire-bulb in place.

3 Now make another 2 holes in the cylinder and secure another wire-bulb. Wrap an elastic band around the top where the wires cross over to fix. Repeat with the other 2 pieces of wire.

4 Weave the horizontal struts with thinner wire by wrapping it around each vertical strut as you go.

5 Cut out individual squares of crepe paper (you can use one colour or several) and glue them on to the wire frame until the *bulb* is covered.

Place your lightbulb-shade over an up-ended torch for a great effect.

Who discovered radium?

Marie Curie (1867-1934) and her husband Pierre (1859-1906) were both physicists. Together, they studied radioactivity, or the radiation given off by certain substances. They also discovered new elements, including radium. In 1904, they were jointly awarded the Nobel Prize.

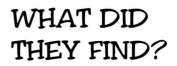

Marie Sklodowska was born in Poland. A brilliant pupil, she won a gold medal when she finished high school, and went on to become a teacher.

Later, she moved to Paris to study physics at the university. She often worked far into the night, living on just bread and butter, and tea.

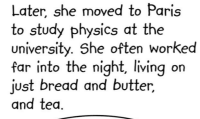

Tell me, Pierre. Do you think the strange rays coming from uranium can be found in other things?

After finishing her studies, Marie began work in a research laboratory, where she met Pierre Curie. They married in 1895 and began a famous partnership. It all started with Marie's deep interest with mysterious rays.

WHAT DID THEY FIND?

- Marie was fascinated by the rays, or signals, coming from the element uranium. They had been discovered by Henri Becquerel in 1896. Did other substances give off similar rays?

- The Curies found strong signals coming from a rock made up of different substances called pitchblende.

- Neither could think where the rays were coming from in the pitchblende. Was there an element in it no one knew about?

- After breaking down the pitchblende with chemicals, they found a new element. But it wasn't the one giving off the mysterious rays!

At long last – a breakthrough! And now, after many nights in the lab and non-stop experimenting, we've also found the element that's giving off the rays. They're so strong, the element glows in the dark. Let's call it radium!

The Curies called the element they found, polonium, named after Marie's homeland. Both polonium and radium were discovered in 1898.

Radioactivity

Marie and Pierre Curie's greatest discovery was finding the two elements **polonium** and **radium**. This led to the inventions of x-ray technology and atomic power. They knew that uranium gave off a strange kind of energy in the form of rays. Marie later called this energy **radiation**. But they were determined to find other sources.

The Curies found that **thorium**, another element, was radioactive. But more importantly, they found very strong radioactivity in pitchblende. Their task was to break down the pitchblende and find out where the radiation was coming from. This took many experiments, but finally Marie was able to isolate radium as the source.

Medical uses

After the death of Pierre in 1906, Marie Curie devoted her life to making the best use of radium. She was determined that it should be used in medicine to help the sick. For this reason it was necessary for her to study the chemistry of radioactive substances, or what they were made up of. In recognition of her work, she was awarded a second Nobel Prize in 1911.

One of her priorities was to make sure there was enough radium for medical use as well as for the experiments she and others were doing at the time. It doesn't seem much, but 1.5g of radium allowed successful experiments to be done for several years. With the help of her daughter Irene, she also worked to develop the use of x-rays as a way of diagnosing illness. Unfortunately, the dangers of radiation were not realised at the time, and Marie died of leukemia, probably caused by radiation poisoning, in 1934.

IMPORTANT NUMBERS

An element such as radium is a substance that cannot be be split into simpler substances by chemical reaction. Each atom in an element has the same number of electrons, known as its atomic number. Radium is 88. The first 95 can all be found in nature. But those with atomic numbers above 95 are artificial. You can often tell these by their name. Element 105 for example, is called Rutherfordium.

Radiography uses x-rays to take pictures that show the insides of our bodies.

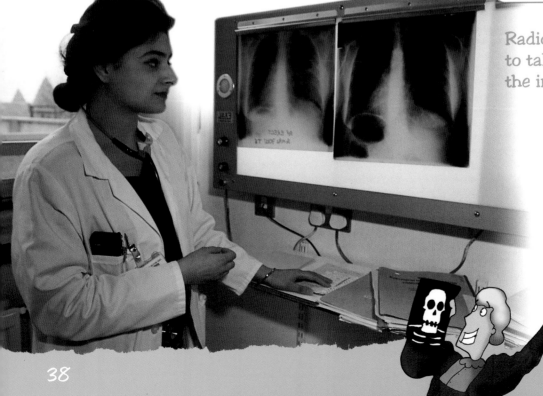

Inventor's words

polonium
radiation
radioactive
radium
thorium
x-ray

Make a spooky skull mask

You will need
- balloon • PVA glue
- newspaper strips
- scissors • pencil
- tissue paper
- clay • elastic band
- black and white paints and brush
- cocktail sticks
- glow paint

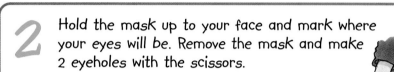

1 Cover half of the balloon with layers of newspaper strips soaked in PVA glue. When dry, pop the balloon and trim the edges of the mask.

2 Hold the mask up to your face and mark where your eyes will be. Remove the mask and make 2 eyeholes with the scissors.

3 Using tissue paper soaked in PVA glue, mould the shape of a skull, building up the layers so the skull shape stands out over the newspaper shell.

4 Make teeth out of pieces of clay. Decorate the mask and give it a coat of glow paint.

5 Make 2 holes in the back of the mask and fix an elastic band to either side with 2 cocktail sticks.

39

Who worked out flight control?

The Wright brothers, Wilbur (1867-1912) and Orville (1871-1948), were aviation pioneers who also built their own machines. They experimented first with gliders, before moving on to powered aircraft. In 1903, Orville made history by flying the world's first power-driven aeroplane.

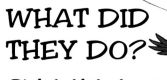

Orville and Wilbur were the sons of a bishop. They both had an aptitude for mechanics, which interested them more than Church activities.

They began by designing and building printing machines. But soon they were making their own bicycles. Their business earned them good money.

The death of Otto Lilienthal in 1896, who had made over 2000 flights in gliders, inspired them. Aerodynamics and engine design were developing rapidly. With their engineering skills, the Wrights were well suited to building a flying machine.

How can we find a way of controlling the airplane once it's in the air, so we can fly in any direction?

WHAT DID THEY DO?

- Birds held the key to the answer. So, the Wright brothers began to study buzzards.

- They wanted to know how buzzards kept their balance in the air. After all, like planes, birds were heavier than air. Why didn't they suddenly tip over and fall to the ground?

- Bird-watching taught them that an aeroplane had to be able to do three things: bank from side to side; climb and descend; and steer left and right. Sometimes it had to be able to do two or all of these things at the same time.

- They soon realised that buzzards flew by twisting their wings in the air.

Wings that move are crucial. We'll make ones that can twist mechanically. This will create more or less lift on one side. A plane will be able to bank for a turn, or roll up or down to regain position. Now we're getting there!

The Wright Brother's bi-plane gliders paved the way to the first manned flight.

Three controls

The Wright brothers are famous for making the first powered aeroplane fly, but their great invention was the **three axes control** of the plane. Every aircraft built since then has the ability to roll or **bank** the wings right or left; to **pitch** the nose up or down; and to yaw the nose to either side. In order to perfect aeroplane control, the Wrights first built three gliders.

The third one, flown at Kill Devil Hills in North Carolina in 1902, was fully controllable. It had a forward **elevator**, or flap, for pitch, a rear rudder for turning left and right and twisting wings for roll. It was tested first in a wind tunnel and then in the air, where it soared to more than 180m. Once the glider was perfected, manned flight was ready to begin.

Up and away

Once Orville and Wilbur had perfected aeroplane control – with the help of the buzzards – they turned to the problem of how to power it. The petrol engine was being used in automobiles, so it was their first choice. However, it proved much too heavy for the plane the Wright brothers planned on constructing.

The answer was to design and build their own engine, which they did. But now they had a power source, they had to think about how the plane would move. The brothers investigated propellers. They reckoned that for an aircraft, a propellor was a moving wing that would drive the plane forwards. The propeller would be turned by the engine. So as long as there was moving air, the plane had power. Their first plane was 'Flyer I' and it made its historic flight on 17 December 1903.

PROTECTION PLAN

Flyer III was the first practical plane built by the Wrights. It could turn, bank, circle and even fly figures of eight. This was just two years after their very first plane had flown. But the Wright brothers kept their work secret and didn't fly again until May 1908. They wanted to patent their inventions before anyone else had a chance, then sell them to a company or the army.

One of the Wright brothers' later aeroplanes.

Inventor's words

banking
elevator
petrol engine
pitch • propellers
three axes
control

Model your own bi-plane

You will need

- white cardboard • scissors
- strong glue • kebab sticks
- cocktail sticks
- empty toilet roll
- egg carton
- stiff coloured card
- plastic spoon
- large plastic bottle lid
- polystyrene cup
- lolly sticks

1 Cut out 2 large wing shapes from cardboard. Glue on *kebab* struts at regular intervals.

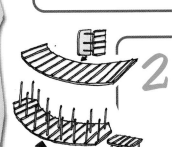

2 Take 16 cocktail sticks and set the wing pieces together with lots of glue. Repeat this process to make a smaller tailpiece and a forward steering device.

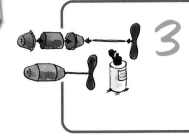

3 Make 2 engines from a toilet roll, the compartments of an egg carton and a *kebab* stick. Now make 2 propellers from card and glue together.

4 Make a seat from a plastic spoon stuck to a bottle lid with card legs. Cut the bottom off a polystyrene cup and glue 2 lolly sticks to the base to make landing skids for the plane.

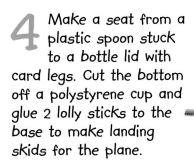

5 Assemble all the parts of the plane and glue well. Use props to hold everything together until the glue sets.

Glossary and index

Aerial Part of a telecommunications system that transmits or receives radio signals. It can be a long piece of wire, a rod or a dish. p.17

Aerodynamics Study of the forces that act on an object as it moves through the air. It is used in the design of aircraft, cars and other means of transport. p.9

Arc light Light that comes from an electric spark in the form of an arc that crosses between two conductors. Arc light was used for street lamps. p.33

Banking To tilt to one side while going round a curve. A plane banks, or tilts its wings, as it turns. p.41

Bed Part of a printing press. It is a flat tray into which blocks of type are fitted. p.13

Block Block of wood used in old printing presses, on which a piece of metal type is fixed. p.13

Calculus System of calculating or reasoning, first used to find rates of change of quantities. Now it is used in mechanics and geometry in relation to curves. p.6

Carrier wave Radio waves at a certain fixed frequency sent out by a radio transmitter. The sound to be sent by the transmitter is changed into electrical signals and combined with the carrier wave. p.18

Dynamo Machine with a shaft that spins, which is used to send an electric current through an electric circuit. p.25

Electric light bulb A glass vacuum bulb, or one with the air taken out. A tiny string of carbon inside the bulb glows when a current is passed through it. p.33

Electromagnetic waves Waves of radiation, including light waves, radio waves, x-rays and gamma rays, which make up the electromagnetic spectrum. p.17

Elevator Moveable part on the tail that allows a plane to alter its pitch. p.41

Exhaustion Complete loss of strength. p.6

Forme Even line of type locked together by quoins, or wedges, to make up a unit. p.14

Frequency The number of electromagnetic waves, such as radio waves, per second. p.18

Generator Type of dynamo. p.25

Graphophone Record player invented by Alexander Graham Bell. It used a wax cylinder and discs with an engraver's stylus. p.30

High-pressure steam engine Small steam engine in which steam was kept under high pressure. It was more efficient than earlier, larger steam engines. p.21

Hydroelectricity Electricity created from the movement of water through a turbine. p.26

Radium Radioactive element. It is a metal found in ores such as pitchblende. p.37

Range To lay type in a row of letters. p.14

Ratchet Toothed device that allows one-way movement only. p.9

Renaissance The Renaissance, which means 'rebirth', that took place in Europe in the late Middle Ages. People were making new discoveries and re-learning old, forgotten ideas and skills. The arts, science, engineering and medicine all flourished. p.10

Scribe Ancient or medieval copyist of manuscripts. p.13

Telegraph Machine that sends messages over a long distance, using a code of long and short electrical pulses along a wire. p.29

Telephone Device for communicating over a distance or out of the hearing range of another person. It has a mouthpiece for turning sound waves into electronic signals, and an earpiece that turns the signals back into sound. p.29

Thorium Radioactive element used as a nuclear fuel. Thorium is thought to be partly responsible for the heat generated inside the Earth. p.37

Three-axis control System used by the Wright brothers to control banking, pitch and steering in a plane. p.41

Type mould Mould used to make metal type. p.14

Vacuum bulb Glass bulb with the air removed from it. p.33

Vibrate Move quickly and continually to and fro. The rate of vibration is measured as frequency. p.29

Volume The volume of space inside an object is measured as a cubic unit. Fluids are measured in litres. p.5

Wireless telegraphy Alexander Graham Bell's description of the first radio. p.17

X-ray Electromagnetic wave with a short wavelength. X-rays have great energy and can travel through some materials such as skin and flesh. They can be used to help treat disease. They are also the photographs made by an x-ray machine. p.38

Tools and Materials

Almost all of the materials in this book can be found around the house or bought at your local art or craft shop. If you cannot find the exact item, try and replace it with something similar.

Most of the models will stick fast with PVA glue or even wallpaper paste. However, some materials need a stronger glue, so take care when using these as they may damage your clothes and even your skin. Ask an adult to help you.

Always cover furniture with newspaper or a large cloth, and protect your clothes by wearing a work apron.

User Care

Take special care when handling sharp tools such as scissors, pointed gadgets, pieces of wire or craft knives. Ask an adult to help you when you need to use them.